In Honor of a Loyal Friend

Presented By

BB

Prayers of a Loyal Friend

Dr. Criswell Freeman

31 Days Celebrating Christian Friendship

BB

Brighton Books
Nashville, TN

Prayers of a Loyal Friend

Dr. Criswell Freeman

31 Days Celebrating Christian Friendship

Brighton Books
Nashville, TN 37204

ISBN 1-58334-129-3

The quoted ideas expressed in this book (but not scripture verses) are not, in all cases, exact quotations, as some have been edited for clarity and brevity. In all cases, the author has attempted to maintain the speaker's original intent. In some cases, quoted material for this book was obtained from secondary sources, primarily print media. While every effort was made to ensure the accuracy of these sources, the accuracy cannot be guaranteed. For additions, deletions, corrections or clarifications in future editions of this text, please write BRIGHTON BOOKS.

Printed in the United States of America
Cover Design & Page Layout: *Bart Dawson*

1 2 3 4 5 6 7 8 9 10 • 02 03 04 05 06 07 08 09 10

In Memory of:
Rick Hutton
(1955-2002)

He was a friend to all who knew him.
A caring, thoughtful, and loyal friend.

Table of Contents

Help Me, Lord...

How to Use This Book

Loyal Christian friendship is ordained by God. Throughout the Bible, we are reminded to love one another, to care for one another, and to treat one another as we wish to be treated. This collection of devotional readings is a celebration of Christian friendship. As such, it is intended to help you in your efforts to be the kind of friend that God intends.

Daily life is woven together with the threads of habit, and no habit is more important to your spiritual growth than the discipline of daily prayer and devotion to God. This text is divided into 31 chapters, one for each day of the month. Each chapter contains Bible verses, quotations, brief essays, and prayers, all dealing with various aspects of Christian friendship. During the next 31 days, please try this experiment: Read one chapter each day. If you're already committed to a daily worship time, this book will enrich that experience. If you are not, the simple act of giving God a few minutes each morning will change the tone and direction of your life.

Because you have taken time to open this book and begin reading, you understand the important role that Christian friendship plays in God's plans for His kingdom *and* for your life. Christ promises His followers a life of abundance *(John 10:10)*. May your friends bless *you* abundantly, and may you do the same *for them*.

This is my commandment,
That ye love one another,
as I have loved you. Greater love
hath no man than this, that a man lay
down his life for his friends.

—

John 15:12-13 KJV

Help Me, Lord... To Share Christ's Love

Who will separate us from the love of Christ? Will tribulation, or distress, or persecution, or famine, or nakedness, or peril, or sword? But in all these things we overwhelmingly conquer through Him who loved us.

Romans 8:35,37 NASB

The old familiar hymn begins, "What a friend we have in Jesus..." No truer words were ever penned. Jesus is the sovereign friend and ultimate savior of mankind. Christ showed His love for believers by willingly sacrificing His own life so that we might have eternal life: *But God demonstrates his own love for us in this: While we were still sinners, Christ died for us.* *(Romans 5:8 NIV)* We, as Christ's followers, are challenged to share His love.

When we accept Christ as our savior, we become ambassadors for Him. *(II Corinthians 5:20)* And when we walk each day with Jesus—and obey the commandments found in God's Holy Word—we are not only *worthy* ambassadors, we are also *trustworthy* friends.

Just as Christ has been—and will always be—the ultimate friend to His flock, so should we be Christ-like in our love and devotion to *our own* little flock of friends and neighbors. When we share the love of Christ, we share a priceless gift. As loyal friends, we must do no less.

The secret of the Christian is that he knows the absolute deity of the Lord Jesus Christ.

Oswald Chambers

Christ is like a river in another respect. A river is continually flowing, there are fresh supplies of water coming from the fountain-head continually, so that a man may live by it, and be supplied with water all his life. So Christ is an ever-flowing fountain; he is continually supplying his people, and the fountain is not spent. They who live upon Christ may have fresh supplies from him to all eternity; they may have an increase of blessedness that is new, and new still, and which never will come to an end.

Jonathan Edwards

Jesus Christ is the first and last, author and finisher, beginning and end, alpha and omega, and by Him all other things hold together. He must be first or nothing. God never comes next!

Vance Havner

Jesus made Himself known to His own, and if others are to hear about him today, you and I must tell them.

Vance Havner

Today's Prayer

Thank You, Lord, for Your Son Jesus, the Savior of my life. You loved this world so dearly, Lord, that you sent Your Son to die so that we, your children, might have life eternal. Let me be ever grateful for that priceless gift, and let the love of Jesus be reflected in my words, my thoughts, and my deeds. Let me always count Jesus as my dearest friend, and let me share His transforming message with a world in desperate need of His peace.

Amen

Help Me, Lord... To Show Kindness

> A kind man benefits himself, but a cruel man brings trouble on himself.
>
> *Proverbs 11:17 NIV*

The noted American theologian Phillips Brooks advised, "Be such a man, and live such a life, that if every man were such as you, and every life a life like yours, this earth would be God's Paradise." One tangible way to make the world a more godly place is to spread kindness wherever we go.

For Christian believers, kindness is not an option, it is a commandment. In the Gospel of Matthew, Jesus declares, *In everything, therefore, treat people the same way you want them to treat you, for this is the Law and the Prophets. (Matthew 7:12 NASB)* Jesus did not say, "In some things, treat people as you wish to be treated." And, He did not say, "From time to time, treat others with kindness." Christ said that we should treat others as we wish to be treated *in everything*. This, of course, is a tall order indeed, but as Christians, we are commanded to do our best.

Today, as you consider all the things that Christ has done in your life, honor Him by being a little kinder than necessary. Honor Him by slowing down long enough to say an extra word of encouragement to someone who needs it. Honor Him by picking up the phone and calling a distant friend...for no reason other than to say, "I'm thinking of you." Honor Christ by following His commandment and obeying the Golden Rule. He expects no less, and He deserves no less.

Be gentle unto all men, apt to teach, patient.

II Timothy 2:24 KJV

Do all the good you can. By all the means you can. In all the ways you can. In all the places you can. At all the times you can. To all the people you can.

John Wesley

We hurt people by being too busy to notice their needs.

Billy Graham

It is the duty of every Christian to be Christ to his neighbor.

Martin Luther

He who is filled with love is filled with God Himself.

St. Augustine

Today's Prayer

Heavenly Father, sometimes this world can become a demanding place, a place where I rush through the day with my eyes focused only on my next step. Give me wisdom and peace, Lord, so that I might look beyond my own needs and see the needs of those around me. Today, help me to be generous, compassionate, and understanding. Today, let me spread kind words and deeds to all who cross my path. Today, let the love for Christ shine through me. And let me show kindness to all who need the healing touch of our Master's hand.

Amen

Help Me, Lord... To Be Patient

> We urge you, brethren, admonish
> the unruly, encourage the
> fainthearted, help the weak,
> be patient with everyone.
>
> *I Thessalonians 5:14 NASB*

Friendship requires patience. From time to time, even our most considerate friends may do things that worry us, or confuse us, or anger us. Why do even the most loyal friends frustrate us on occasion? Because they are human. And it is precisely *because* they are human that we must, from time to time, be patient with their shortcomings (just as they, too, must be patient with ours).

Patience is God's way. Lamentations 3:25-26 reminds us that, *The Lord is wonderfully good to those who wait for him and seek him. So it is good to wait quietly for salvation from the Lord.* (NIV) But, for most of us, waiting quietly for God is difficult. Why? Because we, like our friends, are fallible human beings, sometimes quick to anger and sometimes slow to forgive.

The next time you find yourself drumming your fingers while waiting for a friend to do the right thing, take a deep breath and ask God for patience. After all, the world unfolds according to God's timetable, not ours. And our friends live—and grow—according to their own timetables, too. Sometimes, we must wait patiently, and that's as it should be. After all, think how patient God has been with us.

Better a patient man than a warrior,
a man who controls his temper than
one who takes a city.

Proverbs 16:32 NIV

Give me such love for God and men
as will blot out all bitterness.

Dietrich Bonhoeffer

A man's wisdom gives him patience;
it is to his glory to overlook an offense.

Proverbs 19:11 NIV

To wait upon God is the perfection of activity.

Oswald Chambers

Today's Prayer

Lord, This world can be a demanding place indeed, and I am tempted to rush through my day scarcely giving a thought to the blessings You have given me. There seem to be so many things to accomplish and so little time, Lord, and I am often impatient with friends, with family, and even with myself. Slow me down, Dear Lord, and help me to live on Your timetable, not my own. Keep me mindful that the world is Your creation and that it unfolds according to Your plans. Let me trust Your plans, Lord, with patience and thanksgiving, today and always.

Amen

Help Me, Lord... To Be Generous

> Verily I say unto you, Inasmuch as ye have done it unto one of the least of these my brethren, ye have done it unto me.
>
> *Matthew 25:40 KJV*

The thread of generosity is woven—completely and inextricably—into the very fabric of Christ's teachings. As He sent His disciples out to heal the sick and spread God's message of salvation, Jesus offered this guiding principle: *Freely you have received, freely give. (Matthew 10:8 NIV)* The principle still applies. If we are to be disciples of Christ, we must give freely of our time, our possessions, and our love.

In II Corinthians 9, Paul reminds us that when we sow the seeds of generosity, we reap bountiful rewards in accordance with God's plan for our lives. Thus, we are instructed to give cheerfully and without reservation: *But this I say, He which soweth sparingly shall reap also sparingly; and he which soweth bountifully shall reap also bountifully. Every man according as he purposeth in his heart, so let him give; not grudgingly, or of necessity: for God loveth a cheerful giver. (v. 6, 7 KJV)*

Today, make this pledge and keep it: Be a cheerful, generous, courageous giver. The world needs your help, and *you* need the spiritual rewards that will be yours when you do.

Jesus had an unselfish heart. If he lives in us, selfishness will not predominate.

Billy Graham

Freely you have received, freely give.

Matthew 10:8 NIV

We are never more like God than when we give.

Chuck Swindoll

And above all things have fervent charity among yourselves: for charity shall cover the multitude of sins.

I Peter 4:8 KJV

Today's Prayer

Heavenly Father, You have blessed me with a love that is far beyond my limited understanding; You sent Your Son Jesus to redeem me from my sins; You have given me the gift of eternal life. Let me be thankful, and let me praise You always. Today, let me share the countless blessings that I have received. Let me share my joy, my possessions, and my faith with others. And, let me be a humble giver, Lord, so that all the glory might be Yours today and forever.

Amen

Help Me, Lord... To Encourage Others

But encourage one another day after day, as long as it is still called "Today," so that none of you will be hardened by the deceitfulness of sin.

Hebrews 3:13 NASB

Part of the art of friendship is learning the skill of encouraging others. And make no mistake: Encouragement is a skill that is learned over time and improved with constant use. As Christians, we are called upon to encourage one another, but sometimes we're not sure exactly what to say or do. How, we ask, can we be most encouraging? The answer is found, in part, by reminding ourselves of what genuine encouragement *is* and what it *is not*.

The dictionary defines encouragement as "the act of inspiring courage and confidence." As Christians, we must first seek to inspire others' confidence in God and in His Son Jesus Christ. We are comforted by the knowledge that God's gifts are too numerous to count and that His love extends to all generations—including our own. While our greatest encouragement comes from the assurance of God's power and His promises, we can also find encouragement when we are reminded of *our own* abilities and strengths. Genuine encouragement is not idle flattery; it is simply a firm reminder of talents that God has given each of us and of our need to use those talents wisely.

Genuine encouragement should never be confused with pity. God intends for His children to lead lives of abundance, joy, celebration and praise—not lives of self-pity or regret. So we must guard ourselves against hosting *or* joining the "pity parties"

that so often accompany difficult times. Instead, we must encourage each other to have faith—first in God and his only begotten Son—and then in our own abilities to use the talents God has given us for the furtherance of His kingdom and for the betterment of our own lives.

Encouragement is the oxygen of the soul.

John Maxwell

How many people stop because so few say, "Go!"

Chuck Swindoll

A lot of people have gone further than they thought they could because someone else thought they could.

Zig Ziglar

Today's Prayer

Dear Heavenly Father, because I am Your child, I am blessed. You have loved me eternally, cared for me faithfully, and saved me through the gift of Your Son Jesus. Just as You have lifted me up, Lord, let me also lift up others in a spirit of encouragement, and optimism, and hope. Today, and every day, let me share the healing message of Your Son, and let me leave this world a little better than I found it, whether through a genuine smile, a firm handshake, a kind word, or a heartfelt prayer.

Amen

Help Me, Lord... To Forgive

And be ye kind one to another, tenderhearted, forgiving one another, even as God for Christ's sake hath forgiven you.

Ephesians 4:32 KJV

Forgiveness is God's commandment, but oh how difficult a commandment it can be to follow. Being frail, fallible, imperfect human beings, we are quick to anger, quick to blame, slow to forgive, and even slower to forget. But, forgiveness, no matter how difficult, is God's way, and it must be our way, too.

God's commandments are not intended to be customized for the particular whims of particular believers. God's word is not a menu from which each of us may select items à la carte, according to our own desires—far from it. God's Holy Word is a book that must be taken in its entirety; all of God's commandments are to be taken seriously. And, so it is with forgiveness.

If, in your heart, you hold bitterness against even a single person, forgive. If there exists even one person, alive or dead, whom you have not forgiven, follow God's commandment and His will for your life: forgive. If you are embittered against yourself for some past mistake or shortcoming, forgive yourself. Then, to the best of your abilities, forget. And move on. Hatred and bitterness and regret are not part of God's plan for your life. Forgiveness is.

Forgiveness is God's command.

Martin Luther

To forgive the incessant provocations of daily life—to keep on forgiving the bossy mother-in-law, the bullying husband, the nagging wife, the selfish daughter, the deceitful son—how can we do it? Only, I think, by remembering where we stand, by meaning our words when we say in our prayers each night, "Forgive us our trespasses as we forgive those that trespass against us." We are offered forgiveness on no other terms. To refuse it is to refuse God's mercy for ourselves. There is no hint of exceptions and God means what he says.

C. S. Lewis

Jesus had a forgiving and understanding heart. If he lives within us, mercy will temper our relationships with our fellow men.

Billy Graham

Blessed are the merciful: for they shall obtain mercy.

Matthew 5:7 KJV

Today's Prayer

Heavenly Father, forgiveness is Your commandment, and I know that I must forgive others just as You have forgiven me. But genuine, lasting forgiveness is difficult. Help me to forgive those who have injured me, and deliver me from the traps of anger and bitterness. Sometimes, I feel the strong desire to strike out against those who have hurt me, but You command me to turn away from revenge. Keep me mindful, Lord, that I am never fully liberated until I have been freed from the prison of hatred and anger—and that You offer me that freedom through Your Son, Jesus Christ.

Amen

Help Me, Lord... To Be an Example of Right Actions

> Blessed is the man that walketh
> not in the counsel of the ungodly,
> nor standeth in the way of sinners,
> nor sitteth in the seat of
> the scornful.
>
> *Psalm 1:1 KJV*

Oswald Chambers, the author of the Christian classic devotional text *My Utmost For His Highest*, advised, "Never support an experience which does not have God as its source, and faith in God as its result." These words serve as a powerful reminder that, as Christians, we are called to walk with God and obey His commandments. But, we live in a world that presents us with countless temptations to stray far from God's path. We Christians, when confronted with sin, have clear instructions: Walk—or better yet run—in the opposite direction.

When we seek righteousness in our own lives—and when we seek the companionship of those who do likewise—we reap the spiritual rewards that God intends for our lives. When we behave ourselves as godly men and women, we honor God. When we live righteously and according to God's commandments, He blesses us in ways that we cannot fully understand.

Today, take every step of your journey with God as your traveling companion. Read His Word and follow His commandments. Support only those activities that further God's kingdom *and* your spiritual growth. Be an example of righteous living to your friends, to your neighbors, and to your children. Then, reap the blessings that God has promised to all those who live according to His will and His word.

And we pray this in order that you may live a life worthy of the Lord and may please him in every way: bearing fruit in every good work, growing in the knowledge of God.

Colossians 1:10 NIV

He leads us in the paths of righteousness wherever we are placed.

Oswald Chambers

Hope to the end for the grace that is to be brought unto you at the revelation of Jesus Christ; as obedient children, not fashioning yourselves according to the former lusts in your ignorance....

I Peter 1:13-14 KJV

Resolved: never to do anything which I should be afraid to do if it were the last hour of my life.

Jonathan Edwards

Today's Prayer

Lord, this world is filled with temptations, distractions, and frustrations. When I turn my thoughts away from You and Your Word, Lord, I suffer. But when I trust in Your commandments, when I turn my thoughts, my faith, and my prayers to You, I am safe. Let me live according to Your commandments. Direct my path far from the temptations and distractions of the world. Let me discover Your will and follow it, Dear Lord, this day and always.

Amen

Help Me, Lord... To Share Your Peace

Peace I leave with you, my peace I give unto you: not as the world giveth, give I unto you. Let not your heart be troubled, neither let it be afraid.

John 14:27 KJV

The beautiful words of *John 14:27* give us hope: *Peace I leave with you, my peace I give unto you....* Jesus offers us peace, not as the world gives, but as He alone gives. We, as believers, can accept His peace or ignore it.

When we accept the peace of Jesus Christ into our hearts, our lives are transformed. And then, because we possess the gift of peace, we can share that gift with fellow Christians, family members, friends, and associates. If, on the other hand, we choose to ignore the gift of peace—for whatever reason—we cannot share it with others.

Today, as a gift to yourself, to your family, and to your friends, claim the inner peace that is your spiritual birthright: the peace of Jesus Christ. It is offered freely; it has been paid for in full; it is yours for the asking. So ask. And then share.

When we learn to say a deep, passionate yes
to the things that really matter...
then peace begins to settle onto our lives like
golden sunlight sifting to a forest floor.

Thomas Kinkade

He keeps us in perfect peace while
He whispers His secrets and
reveals His counsels.

Oswald Chambers

There may be no trumpet sound or loud applause
when we make a right decision,
just a calm sense of resolution and peace.

Gloria Gaither

And let the peace of God rule in your hearts...
and be ye thankful.

Colossians 3:15 KJV

Today's Prayer

Lord, when I turn my thoughts and prayers to You, I feel the peace that You intend for my life. But sometimes, Lord, I distance myself from You; sometimes, I am distracted by the busyness of the day or the demands of the moment. When I am worried or anxious, Lord, turn my thoughts back to You. You are the Giver of all things good, Dear Lord, and You give me peace when I draw close to You. Help me to trust Your will, to follow Your commands, and to accept Your peace, today and forever.

Amen

Help Me, Lord... To Be a Friend in Adversity

I took my troubles to the Lord;
I cried out to him and he
answered my prayer.
Psalm 120:1 NLT

On occasion, all of us face adversity. Throughout the seasons of life, we must all endure life-altering personal losses that leave us breathless. When we do, God stands ready to protect us. Psalm 147 promises, *He heals the brokenhearted, and binds their wounds.* (v. 3 NASB) God keeps His promises. When we are troubled, we can call upon Him, and—in His own time and according to His own plan—He will heal us.

Sometimes, of course, it is not we, but instead our friends, who face adversity. When friends or family members face troubling times, our mission, as Christians, is simple: We must assist in any way we can, either with an encouraging word, a helping hand, or a heartfelt prayer.

The English clergyman Charles Kingsley had practical advice for Christian friends of every generation. He advised, "Make it a rule, and pray to God to help you to keep it, never, if possible, to lie down at night without being able to say: 'I have made one human being at least a little wiser, or a little happier, or at least a little better this day.'" Amen to that...especially in times of adversity.

It is one thing to love the ways of the Lord when all is well and quite another thing to cling to them during discouragement or difficulty.

C. H. Spurgeon

Down through the centuries, in times of trouble and trial, God has brought courage to the hearts of those who love Him. The Bible is filled with assurances of God's help and comfort in every kind of trouble which might cause fears to arise in the human heart. You can look ahead with promise, hope, and joy.

Billy Graham

God allows us to experience the low points of life in order to teach us lessons that we could learn in no other way.

C. S. Lewis

Measure the size of the obstacles against the size of God.

Beth Moore

Today's Prayer

Dear Heavenly Father, You are my strength and my protector. When I am troubled, You comfort me. When I am discouraged, You lift me up. When I am afraid, You deliver me. Let me turn to You, Lord, when I am weak. In times of adversity, let me trust Your plan and Your will for my life. Your love is infinite, as is Your wisdom. Whatever my circumstances, Dear Lord, let me always give the praise, and the thanks, and the glory to You.

Amen

Help Me, Lord... To Share Your Joy

These things have I spoken unto you, that my joy might remain in you, and that your joy might be full.

John 15:11 KJV

Christ made it clear to His followers: He intended that *His* joy would become *their* joy. And it still holds true today: Christ intends that *His* believers share *His* love with *His* joy in their hearts. Yet, sometimes, amid the inevitable hustle and bustle of life-here-on-earth, we can forfeit—albeit temporarily—the joy of Christ as we wrestle with the challenges of daily living.

C. H. Spurgeon, the renowned 19th-century English clergymen, advised, "The Lord is glad to open the gate to every knocking soul. It opens very freely; its hinges are not rusted; no bolts secure it. Have faith and enter at this moment through holy courage. If you knock with a heavy heart, you shall yet sing with joy of spirit. Never be discouraged!"

If, today, your heart is heavy, open the door of your soul to Christ. He will give you peace and joy. And if you *already* have the joy of Christ in your heart, share it freely, just as Christ freely shared His joy with you.

Happiness depends on what happens;
joy does not.

Oswald Chambers

I choose joy...I will invite God to be the God of circumstance. I will refuse the temptation to be cynical...the tool of a lazy thinker. I will refuse to see people as anything less than human beings, created by God. I will refuse to see any problem as anything less than an opportunity to see God.

Max Lucado

Christ is not only a remedy for your weariness and trouble, but he will give you an abundance of the contrary, joy and delight. They who come to Christ, do not only come to a resting-place after they have been wandering in a wilderness, but they come to a banqueting-house where they may rest, and where they may feast. They may cease from their former troubles and toils, and they may enter upon a course of delights and spiritual joys.

Jonathan Edwards

Claim the joy that is yours. Pray. And know that your joy is used by God to reach others.

Kay Arthur

Today's Prayer

Dear Lord, help me to feel Your joy and to share it. Let me open myself to You, and then, with Your joy in my heart, let me reach out to others. Let this day and every day be a celebration, Lord, of Your grace, Your mercy, and Your love. And let me share the Good News of Your son Jesus with a world that so desperately needs His healing touch.

Amen

Help Me, Lord... To Share a Message of Hope

Be of good courage, and he shall strengthen your heart, all ye that hope in the Lord.

Psalm 31:24 KJV

There are few sadder sights on earth than the sight of a man or woman who has lost all hope. In difficult times, hope can be elusive, but those who place their faith in God's promises need *never* lose it. After all, God is good; His love endures; He has promised His children the gift of eternal life. And, God keeps his promises.

Despite God's promises, despite Christ's love, and despite our countless blessings, we frail human beings can still lose hope from time to time. When we do, we need the encouragement of Christian friends, the life-changing power of prayer, and the healing truth of God's Holy Word.

If you find yourself falling into the spiritual traps of worry and discouragement, seek the healing touch of Jesus and the encouraging words of fellow Christians. If you find a friend in need, remind him or her of the peace that is found through a personal relationship with Christ. It was Christ who promised, *These things I have spoken unto you, that in me ye might have peace. In the world ye shall have tribulation: but be of good cheer; I have overcome the world.* *(John 16:33 KJV)*

This world can be a place of trials and tribulations, but as believers, we are secure. God has promised us peace, joy, and eternal life. And, of course, God keeps His promises today, tomorrow, and forever.

Hope is no other than the expectation of those things which faith has believed to be truly promised by God.

John Calvin

Hope deferred maketh the heart sick....

Proverbs 13:12 KJV

Everything that is done in the world is done by hope.

Martin Luther

But as for me, I will always have hope; I will praise you more and more.

Psalm 71:14 NIV

Today's Prayer

Lord, when my path is steep and my heart is troubled, let me trust in You. When I become discouraged or anxious, let me depend upon You. When I lose faith in this world, let me never lose faith in You. Remind me, Lord, that in every situation and in every season of life, You will love me and protect me. And with You as my protector, I need never lose hope because You, Lord, remain sovereign today and tomorrow, and forever.

Amen

Help Me, Lord...
To Celebrate Life

> This is the day which the Lord
> hath made; we will rejoice
> and be glad in it.
>
> *Psalm 118:24 KJV*

Oswald Chambers correctly observed, "Joy is the great note all throughout the Bible." C. S. Lewis echoed that thought when he wrote, "Joy is the serious business of heaven." But, even the most dedicated Christians can, on occasion, forget to celebrate each day for what it is: a priceless gift from God.

Today, let us celebrate life as God intended. Today, let us share the Good News of Jesus Christ. Today, let us put smiles on our faces, kind words on our lips, and songs in our hearts. Let us be generous with our praise and free with our encouragement. And then, when we have celebrated life to the fullest, let us invite others to do likewise. After all, this is God's day, and He has given us clear instructions for its use. We are commanded to rejoice and be glad. So, with no further ado, let the celebration begin...

Make a joyful noise unto the Lord all ye lands. Serve the Lord with gladness: come before his presence with singing. Know ye that the Lord he is God: it is he that hath made us, and not we ourselves; we are his people and the sheep of his pasture. Enter into his gates with thanksgiving , and into his courts with praise; be thankful unto him and bless his name. For the Lord is good; his mercy is everlasting; and his truth endureth to all generations.

Psalm 100:1-5 KJV

Love, joy, peace, patience, kindness, goodness, faithfulness, gentleness, and self-control. To these I commit my day. If I succeed, I will give thanks. If I fail, I will seek his grace. And then when this day is done, I will place my head on my pillow and rest.

Max Lucado

I will thank you, Lord with all my heart; I will tell of all the marvelous things you have done. I will be filled with joy because of you. I will sing praises to your name, O Most High.

Psalm 9:1-2 NLT

Today's Prayer

Lord God, You have given me so many reasons to celebrate. The heavens proclaim your handiwork, and every star in the sky tells of your power. You sent Your Son to die for my sins, and You gave me the gift of life. Let me be mindful of all my blessings, and let me celebrate You and Your marvelous creation. Let me rejoice in this day and every day, now and forever. Today is Your gift to me, Lord. Let me use it to Your glory while giving all the praise to You.

Amen

Help Me, Lord... To Tell of Your Miracles

For with God nothing shall be impossible.

Luke 1:37 KJV

Much has been written about a harsh economic reality: Too many people live below the "poverty line." But, when we turn our thoughts from economics to religion, we must conclude that we live in a world where *spiritual* poverty is an even greater problem than *fiscal* poverty. How, then, can we assess the level of our spiritual riches, or lack thereof? In part, by measuring the faith we place in God.

Too many Christians live below the "miracle line," mistakenly limiting themselves as they mistakenly limit God. We human beings have a strange disinclination to believe in things that are beyond our meager abilities to understand. We read of God's miraculous works in Biblical times, but we tell ourselves, "That was then, and this is now." When we do so, we are mistaken. God is with His children "now" just as He was "then." He is right here, right now, performing miracles. And, He will continue to work miracles in our lives to the extent we are willing to trust in Him and to the extent those miracles fit into the fabric of His divine plan.

Miracles—both great and small—happen around us all day every day, but usually, we're too busy to notice. Some miracles, like the twinkling of a star or the glory of a sunset, we take for granted. Other miracles, like the healing of a

terminally sick patient, we chalk up to fate or to luck. We assume, quite incorrectly, that God is "out there" and we are "right here." Nothing could be farther from the truth.

Do you lack the faith that God can work miracles in your own life? If so, it's time to reconsider. Are you living *below* the miracle line? If so, you are attempting to place limitations on a God who has none. Instead, trust God, and His power, *and* His miracles. And then wait patiently...something miraculous is about to happen.

We have a God who delights in impossibilities.

Andrew Murray

The impossible is exactly what God does.

Oswald Chambers

Today's Prayer

Heavenly Father, Your infinite power is beyond human understanding. With You, Lord, nothing is impossible. Keep me always mindful of Your power, and let me share the glorious message of Your miracles. When I lose hope, give me faith; when others lose hope, let me tell them of Your glory and Your works. Today, Lord, let me expect the miraculous, let me praise You, and let me give thanks for Your miracles.

Amen

Help Me, Lord... To Be an Example of Faithful Living

> Now the just shall live by faith....
>
> *Hebrews 10:38 KJV*

The author of Hebrews makes his point clearly and forcefully: *the just shall live by faith*. When a suffering woman sought healing by merely touching the hem of His cloak, Jesus replied, *Daughter, be of good comfort; thy faith hath made thee whole.* *(Matthew 9:24 KJV)* The message to believers of every generation is clear: live by faith today and every day. But, when we face adversity, illness, or heartbreak, living by faith can be difficult indeed.

Concentration camp survivor Corrie ten Boom relied on faith during her ten months of imprisonment and torture. Later, despite the fact that four of her family members had died in Nazi death camps, Corrie's faith was unshaken. She wrote, "There is no pit so deep that God's love is not deeper still." Christians take note: Genuine faith in God means faith in all circumstances, happy or sad, joyful or tragic.

If, today, your faith is being tested to the point of breaking, know that Your Savior is near. If you reach out to Him in faith, He will give you peace and heal your broken spirit. Be content to touch even the smallest fragment of the Master's garment, and He will make you whole.

Our faith grows by expression.
If we want to keep our faith,
we must share it.

Billy Graham

Faith is an activity. It is something
that has to be applied.

Corrie ten Boom

The beautiful thing about this adventure
called faith is that we can count on
Him never to lead us astray.

Chuck Swindoll

Grace calls you to get up, throw off your
blanket of helplessness, and to move on
through life in faith.

Kay Arthur

Today's Prayer

Lord, I want to be Your faithful servant.
Guide my thoughts, my words,
and my actions this day and every day.
Let me live each day with an unshakable
faith in You, Lord, trusting You
in every circumstance. And, let me be
an example of faithful living so that
I might be a worthy ambassador
for You and Your beloved Son,
my savior, Christ Jesus.

Amen

Help Me, Lord... To Share in Worship

> But seek ye first the kingdom of God, and his righteousness; and all these things shall be added unto you.
>
> *Matthew 6:33 KJV*

All of mankind is engaged in worship…of one kind or another. The question is not *whether* we worship, but *what* we worship. Some of us choose to worship God. The result is a plentiful harvest of joy, peace, and abundance. Others distance themselves from God by foolishly worshiping things of this earth such as fame, fortune, or personal gratification. To do so is a terrible mistake with eternal consequences.

Whenever we place our love for material possessions above our love for God—or when we yield to the countless temptations of this world—we find ourselves engaged in a struggle between good and evil, a clash between God and Satan. Our responses to these struggles have implications that echo throughout our families and throughout our communities.

How can we ensure that we cast our lot with God? We do so, in part, by the practice of regular worship in the company of fellow believers. When we worship God faithfully and fervently, we are blessed. When we fail to worship God, for whatever reason, we forfeit the spiritual gifts that He intends for us. Every day provides opportunities to put God where He belongs: at the center of our lives. When we do so, we worship not just with our words, but with deeds, and that's as it should be. For believers, God comes first. Always first.

The New Testament does not envisage solitary religion; some kind of regular assembly for worship and instruction is everywhere taken for granted in the Epistles.

C. S. Lewis

In the sanctuary, we discover beauty: the beauty of His presence.

Kay Arthur

Don't ever come to church without coming as though it were the first time, as though it could be the best time, and as though it might be the last time.

Vance Havner

If you will not worship God seven days a week, you do not worship Him on one day a week.

A. W. Tozer

Today's Prayer

Heavenly Father, this world can be a place of distractions and temptations. But when I worship You, Lord, You direct my path and You cleanse my heart. Let today and every day be a time of worship and praise. Let me worship You in everything that I think and do. Thank You, Lord for the priceless gift of Your Son Jesus. Let me be worthy of that gift, and let me give You the praise and the glory forever.

Amen

Help Me, Lord... To Be an Example of Courage

> Be of good courage, and he shall strengthen your heart, all ye that hope in the LORD.
>
> *Psalm 31:24 KJV*

The journey through life takes us through many peaks and valleys. When we reach the mountaintops, we find it easy to praise God and to give thanks. As we reach the crest of the mountain's peak, we trust God's plan. But, when we find ourselves in the dark valleys of life, when we face disappointment and despair, it is so much more difficult to trust God. But, trust Him we must.

As Christians, we can be comforted: Whether we find ourselves at the pinnacle of the mountain or the darkest depths of the valley, God is there. And, we Christians have every reason to live courageously. After all, Christ has already won the ultimate battle on the cross at Calvary. Still, even dedicated Christians may find their courage tested by the inevitable disappointments and tragedies that occur in the lives of believers and non-believers alike.

The next time you find your courage tested to the limit, lean upon God's promises. Trust His Son. Remember that God is always near and that He is your protector and your deliverer. When you are worried, anxious, or afraid, call upon Him. God can handle your troubles infinitely better than you can, so turn them over to Him. Remember that God rules both mountaintops and valleys—with limitless wisdom and love—now and forever.

If my life is surrendered to God, all is well. Let me not grab it back, as though it were in peril in His hand but would be safer in mine!

Elisabeth Elliot

Let me encourage you to continue to wait with faith. God may or may not perform a miracle, but He is trustworthy to touch you and make you whole where there used to be a hole.

Lisa Whelchel

Relying on God has to begin all over again every day as if nothing had yet been done.

C. S. Lewis

Jesus Christ can make the weakest man into a divine champion, fearing nothing.

Oswald Chambers

Today's Prayer

Dear Lord, sometimes I face disappointments and challenges that leave me worried and afraid. When I am fearful, let me seek Your strength. When I am anxious, give me faith. Keep me mindful, Lord, that You are my God. With You by my side, Lord, I have nothing to fear, and with Your Son Jesus as my Savior, I have received the gift of eternal life. Help me to be Your grateful and courageous servant this day and every day.

Amen

Help Me, Lord... To Understand the Needs of Others

Jesus said unto him, Thou shalt love the Lord thy God with all thy heart, and with all thy soul, and with all thy mind. This is the first and great commandment. And the second is like unto it, Thou shalt love thy neighbor as thyself. On these two commandments hang all the law and the prophets.

Matthew 22:37-40 KJV

Neighbors. We know that we are instructed to love them, and yet there's so little time because we think that we're *so* busy. No matter. As Christians, we are commanded by our Lord and Savior Jesus Christ to love our neighbors just as we love ourselves. We are not *asked* to love our neighbors, nor are we *encouraged* to do so. We are *commanded* to love them. Period.

In order to love our neighbors as God intends, we must first slow down long enough to understand their needs. Slowing down, however, is not as simple as it seems. We live in a fast-paced world with pressures and demands that often sap our time and our energy. Sometimes, we may convince ourselves that slowing down is not an option, but we are wrong. Caring for our neighbors must be *our* priority because it is *God's* priority.

This very day, someone you know needs a word of encouragement, or a pat on the back, or a helping hand, or a heartfelt prayer. And, if you don't reach out to your friend, who will? If you don't take the time to understand the needs of your neighbors, who will? If you don't love your brothers and sisters, who will? So, today, look for a neighbor in need...and then do something to help. Father's orders.

What is your focus today? Joy comes when it is Jesus first, others second…then you.

Kay Arthur

Speak up for those who cannot speak for themselves, for the rights of all who are destitute.

Proverbs 31:9 NIV

Since you cannot do good to all, you are to pay special regard to those who, by the accidents of time, or place, or circumstances, are brought into closer connection with you.

St. Augustine

In everything, therefore, treat people the same way you want them to treat you, for this is the Law and the Prophets.

Matthew 7:12 NASB

Today's Prayer

Lord, make me mindful of the needs of others. Even when I feel burdened by the challenges of the day, make me an ambassador of your Son Jesus. Help me to do Your will by seeking first to understand the needs of my friends and neighbors…and then let me help in whatever way I can. Give me the strength and the courage to be a powerful force for good in Your world, Lord, today and every day.

Amen

Help Me, Lord... To Share Your Word

But he answered and said, It is written, Man shall not live by bread alone but by every word that proceedeth out of the mouth of God.

Matthew 4:4 KJV

The Bible is unlike any other book. A. W. Tozer wrote, "The purpose of the Bible is to bring men to Christ, to make them holy and prepare them for heaven. In this it is unique among books, and it always fulfills its purpose."

As Christians, we are called upon to share God's Holy Word with a world in desperate need of His healing hand. The Bible is an invaluable gift, a tool for Christians to use as they share the Good News of their Savior, Christ Jesus. Too many Christians, however, keep their spiritual tool kits tightly closed and out of sight.

Jonathan Edwards advised, "Be assiduous in reading the Holy Scriptures. This is the fountain whence all knowledge in divinity must be derived. Therefore let not this treasure lie by you neglected." God's Holy Word is, indeed, a priceless, one-of-a-kind treasure. Handle it with care, but more importantly, handle it every day.

Nobody ever outgrows Scripture;
the book widens and deepens with our years.

C. H. Spurgeon

God did not write a book and send it by messenger to be read at a distance by unaided minds. He spoke a Book and lives in His spoken words, constantly speaking His words and causing the power of them to persist across the years.

A. W. Tozer

Walking in faith brings you to the Word of God. There you will be healed, cleansed, fed, nurtured, equipped, and matured.

Kay Arthur

...but whosoever will be great among you, let him be your minister; and whosoever will be chief among you, let him be your servant: even as the Son of man came not to be ministered unto, but to minister, and to give his life a ransom for many.

Matthew 20:26-28 KJV

Today's Prayer

Heavenly Father, Your Holy Word is a light unto the world; let me share that Word with all who cross my path. Let me follow in the footsteps of Your Son Jesus and be a fisher of men. Lord, we live in a world that desperately needs Your saving grace. In all that I do, help me be a worthy witness for You as I share the Good News of Your perfect Son and Your perfect Word.

Amen

Help Me, Lord... To Comfort Those in Need

But Jesus immediately said to them:
"Take courage! It is I.
Don't be afraid."

Matthew 14:27 NIV

We live in a world that is, on occasion, a frightening place. Sometimes, we sustain life-changing losses that are so profound and so tragic that it seems we could never recover. But with God's help, and with the help of encouraging family members and friends, we *can* recover.

In times of need, friends comfort friends. Our task, as Christians, is to comfort our families and friends by sharing not only our own courage but also the peace and assurance of our Lord and Savior, Christ Jesus. As the renowned revivalist Vance Havner observed, "No journey is complete that does not lead through some dark valleys. We can properly comfort others only with the comfort wherewith we ourselves have been comforted of God."

In times of adversity, we are all wise to remember the words of Jesus, who, when He walked on the waters, reassured His disciples, saying, *Take courage! It is I. Don't be afraid.* *(Matthew 14:27 NIV)* Then, with Christ on His throne and trusted friends by our sides, we can face our fears with courage and faith.

Is anyone among you suffering?
Then he must pray.

James 5:13 NASB

Our valleys may be filled with foes and tears;
but we can lift our eyes to the hills
to see God and the angels....

Billy Graham

Despair is always the gateway of faith.

Oswald Chambers

...ye shall be sorrowful, but your sorrow
shall be turned into joy.

John 16:20 KJV

Today's Prayer

Dear Lord, This world is sometimes a difficult place, sometimes filled with tears and suffering. Let me give comfort to those in need, and let me share Your love with those who grieve. When I encounter events that I cannot understand, Lord, keep me ever-mindful of Your infinite wisdom and love. When I meet those who mourn, guide my speech. And when I, too, become discouraged, turn my thoughts to Your love and to Your promises. Let me be a beacon of encouragement in a difficult world, and may the glory be Yours forever.

Amen

Help Me, Lord... To Share My Optimism

> The Lord is my light and my salvation; whom shall I fear? The Lord is the strength of my life; of whom shall I be afraid?
>
> *Psalm 27:1 KJV*

Christians have every reason to be optimistic about life. As John Calvin observed, "There is not one blade of grass, there is no color in this world that is not intended to make us rejoice." But, sometimes, rejoicing is the last thing on our minds. Sometimes, we fall prey to worry, frustration, anxiety, or sheer exhaustion...and our hearts become heavy. What's needed is plenty of rest, a large dose of perspective, and God's healing touch, but not necessarily in that order.

A. W. Tozer writes, "Attitude is all-important. Let the soul take a quiet attitude of faith and love toward God, and from there on, the responsibility is God's. He will make good on His commitments." These words remind us that even when the challenges of the day seem daunting, and even when our hearts are broken, God remains steadfast. And, so must we.

Jesus offers us abundance and joy, but He doesn't force abundance and joy upon us; we must claim these gifts for ourselves. Today, why not claim the joy that is rightfully yours in Christ? Why not take time to celebrate God's glorious creation? When you do so, you will think optimistically about yourself and your world...and you can then share your optimism with others. You'll be better for it...and so will they.

I may not be able to change the world I see around me, but I can change the way I see the world within me.

John Maxwell

Life is 10% what happens to you, 90% how you respond to it.

Chuck Swindoll

Make the least of all that goes and the most of all that comes. Don't regret what is past. Cherish what you have. Look forward to all that is to come. And most important of all, rely moment by moment on Jesus Christ.

Gigi Graham Tchividjian

Keep your feet on the ground, but let your heart soar as high as it will. Refuse to be average or to surrender to the chill of your spiritual environment.

A. W. Tozer

Today's Prayer

Heavenly Father, You love me, You care for me, and You protect me. You have given me the priceless gift of eternal life through the sacrifice that Christ made on the cross at Calvary. Because of You, Father, and because of Your Son, I can live each day with celebration in my heart and praise on my lips. Let me always be thankful, and let me share the Good News of Jesus as I turn my thoughts to You this day and always.

Amen

Help Me, Lord... To Pray

> Rejoice evermore. Pray without ceasing. In every thing give thanks: for this is the will of God in Christ Jesus concerning you.
>
> *I Thessalonians 5:16-18 KJV*

On his second missionary journey, Paul started a small church in Thessalonica. A short time later, he penned a letter that was intended to encourage the new believers at that church. Today, almost 2,000 years later, 1st Thessalonians remains a powerful, practical guide for Christian living.

In his letter, Paul advises members of the new church to "pray without ceasing." His advice applies to Christians of every generation. When we weave the habit of prayer into the very fabric of our days, we invite God to become a partner in every aspect of our lives. When we consult God on an hourly basis, we avail ourselves of His wisdom, His strength, and His love. When we pray without ceasing, we enrich our own lives and the lives of those around us.

Today, instead of turning things over in your mind, turn them over to God in prayer. Instead of worrying about your next decision, ask God to lead the way. Don't limit your prayers to meals or bedtime. Pray constantly about things great and small. God is listening, and He wants to hear from you. Now.

If the spiritual life be healthy, under
the full power of the Holy Spirit,
praying without ceasing will be natural.

Andrew Murray

Prayer is not a work that can be allocated
to one or another group in the church.
It is everybody's responsibility;
it is everybody's privilege.

A. W. Tozer

If you want that splendid power in prayer,
you must remain in loving, living, lasting,
conscious, practical, abiding union with
the Lord Jesus Christ.

C. H. Spurgeon

Don't pray when you feel like it;
make an appointment with
the King and keep it.

Corrie ten Boom

Today's Prayer

Dear Lord, Your Holy Word commands me to pray without ceasing. Let me take everything to You in prayer. When I am discouraged, let me pray. When I am lonely, let me take my sorrows to You. When I grieve, let me take my tears to You, Lord, in prayer. And when I am joyful, let me offer up prayers of thanksgiving. In all things great and small, at all times, whether happy or sad, let me seek Your wisdom and Your Grace...in prayer.

Amen

Help Me, Lord... To Speak Righteously

> But I say unto you, That every idle word that men shall speak, they shall give account thereof in the day of judgment. For by thy words thou shalt be justified, and by thy words thou shalt be condemned.
>
> *Matthew 12:36 KJV*

Think...pause...then speak: How wise is the man or woman who can communicate in this way. But all too often, in the rush to have ourselves heard, we speak first and think second...with unfortunate results.

God's Word reminds us that *Reckless words pierce like a sword, but the tongue of the wise brings healing.* (*Proverbs 12:18 NIV*) If we seek to be a source of encouragement to friends and family, then we must measure our words carefully. Words are important: they can hurt or heal. Words can uplift us or discourage us, and reckless words, spoken in haste, cannot be erased.

Today, seek to encourage all who cross your path. Measure your words carefully. Speak wisely, not impulsively. Use words of kindness and praise, not words of anger or derision. Remember that you have the power to heal others or to injure them, to lift others up or to hold them back. When you lift them up, your wisdom will bring healing and comfort to a world that needs both.

Words. Do you fully understand their power? Can any of us really grasp the mighty force behind the things we say? Do we stop and think before we speak, considering the potency of the words we utter?

Joni Eareckson Tada

How forcible are right words!

Job 6:25 KJV

Set a guard, O LORD, over my mouth;
Keep watch over the door of my lips.

Psalm 141:3 NASB

Let your speech always be with grace, as though seasoned with salt, so that you will know how you should respond to each person.

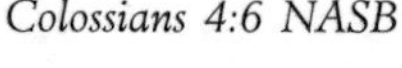
Colossians 4:6 NASB

Today's Prayer

Lord, You have warned me that I will be judged by the words I speak. And You have commanded me to choose my words carefully so that I might be a source of encouragement and hope to all whom I meet. Keep me mindful, Lord, that I have influence on many people...make me an influence for good. And may the words that I speak today be worthy of the One who has saved me forever.

Amen

Help Me, Lord... To Share in Praise

I will praise thee, O LORD, with my whole heart; I will show forth all thy marvelous works. I will be glad and rejoice in thee: I will sing praise to thy name, O thou Most High.

Psalm 9:1-2 KJV

It has been called the most widely-used book of the Old Testament; it is, of course, the book of Psalms. In the Hebrew version of the Old Testament, the title of the book is translated "hymns of praise," and with good reason. Much of the book is a breathtakingly beautiful celebration of God's power, God's love, and God's creation. The psalmist writes *Let everything that has breath praise the Lord. Praise the Lord.* (150:6) As Christians, we should continually praise God for all that He has done and all that he will do. For believers who have accepted the transforming love of Jesus Christ, there is simply no other way.

Today, as you travel to work or school, as you hug your child or kiss your spouse, as you gaze upon a passing cloud or marvel at a glorious sunset, think of what God has done for you, for yours, and for all of us. And, every time you notice a gift from the Giver of all things good, praise Him. His works are marvelous, His gifts are beyond understanding, and His love endures forever.

Praise ye the LORD. O give thanks unto the LORD; for he is good: for his mercy endureth for ever.

Psalm 106:1 KJV

Preoccupy my thoughts with your praise beginning today.

Joni Eareckson Tada

Praise and thank God for who He is and for what He has done for you.

Billy Graham

I will thank you, Lord, in front of all the people. I will sing your praises among the nations. For your unfailing love is higher than the heavens. Your faithfulness reaches to the clouds.

Psalm 108:3 NLT

Today's Prayer

Heavenly Father, Your gifts are greater than I can imagine, and Your love for me is greater than I can fathom. May I live each day with thanksgiving in my heart and praise on my lips. Thank You for the gift of Your Son and for the promise of eternal life. Let me share the joyous news of Jesus Christ with a world that desperately needs His healing touch this day and every day.

Amen

Help Me, Lord...
To Live Humbly

Yea, all of you be subject one to another, and be clothed with humility: for God resisteth the proud, and giveth grace to the humble.

I Peter 5:5 KJV

We have heard the phrase on countless occasions: "He's a self-made man." In truth, none of us are self-made. We all owe countless debts that we can never repay. Our first debt, of course, is to our Father in heaven—Who has given us everything that we are and will ever be—and to His Son Who sacrificed His own life so that we might live eternally. We are also indebted to ancestors, parents, teachers, friends, spouses, family members, coworkers, fellow believers...and the list, of course, goes on.

As Christians, we have a profound reason to be humble: We have been refashioned and saved by Jesus Christ, and that salvation came not because of our own good works but because of God's grace. Thus, we are not "self-made," we are "God-made," and "Christ-saved." How, then, can we be boastful? The answer, of course, is that, if we are honest with ourselves and with our God, we simply cannot be boastful...we must, instead, be eternally grateful and exceedingly humble.

Humility is not, in most cases, a naturally-occuring human trait. Most of us, it seems, are more than willing to stick out our chests and say, "Look at me; I did that!" But in our wiser moments, in the quiet moments when we search the depths of our own hearts, we know better. Whatever "it" is, God did that. And He deserves the credit.

It is very easy to overestimate the importance of our own achievements in comparison with what we owe others.

Dietrich Bonhoeffer

Do you wish to be great? Then begin by being humble. Do you desire to construct a vast and lofty fabric? Think first about the foundations of humility. The higher your structure is to be, the deeper must be its foundation.

St. Augustine

The great characteristic of the saint is humility.

Oswald Chambers

I will boast only in the Lord....

Psalm 34:2 NLT

Today's Prayer

Heavenly Father, it is the nature of mankind to be prideful, and I am no exception. When I am boastful, Lord, keep me mindful that all my gifts come from You. When I feel prideful, remind me that You sent Your Son to be a humble carpenter and that Jesus was ridiculed and crucified on a cross. Let me grow beyond my need for earthly praise, God, and let me look only to You for approval. You are the Giver of all things good; let me give all the glory to You.

Amen

Help Me, Lord... To Live Honestly

The man of integrity walks securely, but he who takes crooked paths will be found out.

Proverbs 10:9 NIV

From the time we are children, we are taught that honesty is the best policy, but sometimes it is *so hard* to be honest and *so easy* to be less than honest. So, we convince ourselves that it's okay to tell "little white lies." But there's a problem: Little white lies tend to grow up, and when they do, they cause havoc and pain in our lives.

For Christian believers, the issue of honesty is not a topic for debate. Honesty is not just the best policy, it is God's policy, pure and simple. If we are to be servants worthy of our Savior, Jesus Christ, we avoid all lies, white or otherwise.

Sometime soon, perhaps even today, you will be tempted to sow the seeds of deception, perhaps in the form of a "harmless" white lie. Resist that temptation. Truth is God's way, and a lie—of whatever color— is not.

Integrity is not a given factor in everyone's life.
It is a result of self-discipline, inner trust,
and a decision to be relentlessly honest
in all situations in our lives.

John Maxwell

A little lie is like a little pregnancy.
It doesn't take long before everyone knows.

C. S. Lewis

...and ye shall know the truth,
and the truth shall make you free.

John 8:32 KJV

Today's Prayer

Lord, truth is Your commandment. You instruct me to seek truth and to live righteously. Help me, Lord, always to live according to Your commandments. Sometimes, Lord, speaking the truth can be difficult indeed, but let me speak forthrightly. And let me walk righteously and courageously so that others might see Your Grace reflected in my words and my deeds.

Amen

Help Me, Lord... To Turn from Sin

...let us throw off everything that hinders and the sin that so easily entangles, and let us run with perseverance the race marked out for us.

Hebrews 12:1 NIV

How hard is it to bump into temptation in this crazy world? Not very hard. The devil, it seems, is working overtime these days, and causing pain and heartache in more places and in more ways than ever before. We, as Christians, must remain vigilant. Not only must we resist Satan when he confronts us, but we must also avoid those places where Satan can most easily tempt us. Clearly, if we are to avoid the unending temptations of this world, we must arm ourselves with the Word of God.

After fasting forty days and nights in the desert, Jesus Himself was tempted by Satan. Christ used scripture to rebuke the devil. *(Matthew 4: 1-11)* We must do likewise. The Holy Bible provides us with a perfect blueprint for righteous living. If we consult that blueprint daily and follow it carefully, we build our lives according to God's plan. But, if we ignore the blueprint or, worse yet, rebel against it, then we suffer tragic consequences.

In a letter to believers, Peter offers a stern warning: *Your adversary, the devil, prowls around like a roaring lion, seeking someone to devour. (I Peter 5:8 NASB)* What was true in New Testament times is equally true in our own. Satan tempts his prey and then devours them. As believing Christians, we must beware. And, if we seek righteousness in our own lives, we must earnestly wrap ourselves in the protection of God's Holy Word. When we do, we are secure.

Christians see sin for what it is: willful rebellion against the rulership of God in their lives. And in turning from their sin, they have embraced God's only means of dealing with sin: Jesus.

Kay Arthur

Measure your growth in grace by your sensitiveness to sin.

Oswald Chambers

Man without God is always torn between two urges. His nature prompts him to do wrong, and his conscience urges him to do right. Christ can rid you of that inner conflict.

Billy Graham

For sin shall not have dominion over you: for ye are not under the law, but under grace.

Romans 6:14 KJV

Today's Prayer

Heavenly Father, the temptation to stray from Your commandments can be as subtle as it is destructive. Because this world contains many traps and snares, I pray for Your wisdom and Your help. Lead me away from temptation, Lord, and deliver me from sin. Today, give me the strength to take every step with You, and let me live according to Your Holy Word. Let my actions and my words be worthy of Your Son Jesus, and let me live in the light of Your righteousness forever.

Amen

Help Me, Lord... To Have a Servant's Heart

The greatest among you will be your servant. For whoever exalts himself will be humbled, and whoever humbles himself will be exalted.

Matthew 23:11 NIV

The teachings of Jesus are crystal clear: We achieve greatness through service to others. But as weak human beings, we sometimes fall short as we seek to puff ourselves up and glorify our own accomplishments. Jesus commands otherwise. He teaches us that the most esteemed men and women are not the self-congratulatory leaders of society but are instead the humblest of servants.

Today, you may feel the temptation to build yourself up in the eyes of your neighbors. Resist that temptation. Instead, serve your neighbors quietly and without fanfare. Find a need and fill it…humbly. Lend a helping hand and share a word of kindness…anonymously, for this is God's way.

As a humble servant, you will glorify yourself not before men, but before God, and that's what God intends. After all, earthly glory is fleeting: here today and all too soon gone. But, heavenly glory endures throughout eternity. So, the choice is yours: Either you can lift yourself up here on earth and be humbled in heaven, or vice versa. Choose vice versa.

Have thy tools ready; God will find thee work.

Charles Kingsley

In God's family, there is to be one great body of people: servants. In fact, that's the way to the top in his kingdom.

Chuck Swindoll

Before the judgment seat of Christ, my service will not be judged by how much I have done but by how much of me there is in it.

A. W. Tozer

Today's Prayer

Dear Lord, in weak moments, I seek to build myself up by placing myself ahead of others. But Your commandment, Lord, is that I become a humble servant to those who need my encouragement, my help, and my love. Create in me a servant's heart. And let me follow in the footsteps of Your Son Jesus who taught us by example that to be great in Your eyes, Lord, is to serve others humbly, faithfully, and lovingly.

Amen

Help Me, Lord... To Help Others See Their Talents

Now there are varieties of gifts, but the same Spirit. And there are varieties of ministries, and the same Lord.

I Corinthians 12: 4-5 NASB

The old saying is both familiar and true: "What we are is God's gift to us; what we become is our gift to God." Each of us possesses special talents, gifted by God, that can be nurtured carefully or ignored totally. Sometimes, we don't fully recognize our own talents, and, sometimes, we don't fully appreciate the gifts we've been given. That's when we need the insights, the support, and the encouragement of trusted friends.

Oswald Chambers observed, "A friend is one who makes me do my best." Our most trusted friends encourage us to set our sights where they need to be set: high. We can do the same for them, and should.

God didn't create us to be mediocre. He gave us talents so that we might use them to the fullest. So, if you're coasting along in neutral, it's time to shift into a higher gear. And, if you know someone whose talents are underused, remind them that those talents are priceless gifts from God, and the way that we say "thank you" for God's gifts is to use them.

Natural abilities are like natural plants;
they need pruning by study.

Francis Bacon

Neglect not the gift that is in thee....

I Timothy 4:14 KJV

One thing taught large in the Holy Scriptures is that while God gives His gifts freely, He will require a strict accounting of them at the end of the road. Each man is personally responsible for his store, be it large or small, and will be required to explain his use of it before the judgment seat of Christ.

A. W. Tozer

He climbs highest who helps another up.

Zig Ziglar

Today's Prayer

Dear Lord, You have blessed all of Your children with special gifts and talents. Let me use my own talents according to Your plan, and help me to encourage others to use theirs. Lord, when we are faithful stewards of our gifts, and when we use those gifts according to Your commandments, we help build Your kingdom. Today, help me to use *all* the talents You have given me, and in turn, let me help others find the strength and courage to use *their* gifts according to Your master plan.

Amen

Help Me, Lord... To Be a Worthy Friend

A friend loves at all times....

Proverbs 17:17 NIV

Friend: a one-syllable word describing "a person who is attached to another by feelings of affection or personal regard." This definition, or one very similar to it, can be found in any dictionary, but genuine friendship is much more. When we examine the deeper meaning of friendship, so many adjectives come to mind: trustworthiness, loyalty, helpfulness, kindness, understanding, forgiveness, encouragement, humor, and cheerfulness, to mention but a few.

Genuine friendship should be treasured and nurtured. As Christians, we are *commanded* to love one another. The familiar words of 1st Corinthians 13:2 remind us that love and charity are among God's greatest gifts: *And though I have the gift of prophecy, and understand all mysteries, and all knowledge; and though I have all faith, so that I could remove mountains, and have not charity, I am nothing.* (KJV)

Today and every day, resolve to be a trustworthy, encouraging, loyal friend. And, treasure the people in your life who are loyal friends to you. Friendship is, after all, a glorious gift, praised by God. Give thanks for that gift and nurture it.

In friendship, God opens your eyes
to the glories of Himself.

Joni Eareckson Tada

The worst solitude is to be destitute
of sincere friendship.

Francis Bacon

Friendship is one of the sweetest joys of life.
Many might have failed beneath
the bitterness of their trial had
they not found a friend.

C. H. Spurgeon

Let us not lose heart in doing good,
for in due time we will reap if we do not grow
weary. So then, while we have opportunity,
let us do good to all people, and especially to
those who are of the household of the faith.

Galatians 6:9-10 NASB

Today's Prayer

Lord, You seek abundance and joy for me and for all Your children. One way that I can share Your joy is through the gift of friendship. Help me to be a loyal friend, Lord. Let me be ready to listen, ready to encourage, and ready to offer a helping hand. Keep me mindful that I am a servant of Your Son Christ Jesus. Let me be a worthy servant, Lord, and a worthy friend. And may the love of Jesus shine through me today and forever.

Amen

Help Me, Lord... To Celebrate Others

A cheerful look brings joy to the heart, and good news gives health to the bones.

Proverbs 15:30 NIV

The 118th Psalm reminds us *This is the day which the Lord hath made; we will rejoice and be glad in it.* (v. 24 KJV) As we rejoice in this day that the Lord has given us, let us remember that an important part of today's celebration is the time we spend celebrating others. Each day provides countless opportunities to encourage others and to praise their good works. When we do, we not only spread seeds of joy and happiness, we also follow the commandments of God's Holy Word.

In his letter to the Ephesians, Paul writes, *Do not let any unwholesome talk come out of your mouths, but only what is helpful for building others up according to their needs, that it may benefit those who listen.* (v. 29 NIV) This passage reminds us that, as Christians, we are instructed to choose our words carefully in order to build others up through wholesome, honest encouragement. How can we encourage others? By celebrating their victories and their accomplishments. As the old saying goes, "When someone does something good, applaud—you'll make two people happy."

Today, look for the good in others and celebrate the good that you find. When you do, you'll be a powerful force of encouragement in the world...and a worthy servant to your God.

Discouraged people don't need critics. They hurt enough already. They don't need more guilt or piled-on distress. They need encouragement. They need a refuge. A willing, caring, available someone.

Chuck Swindoll

...let us consider how to stimulate one another to love and good deeds.

Hebrews 10:24 KJV

God grant we may not hinder those who are battling their way slowly into the light.

Oswald Chambers

A cheerful look brings joy to the heart, and good news gives health to the bones.

Proverbs 15:30 NIV

Today's Prayer

Lord, You have placed countless
people along my path:
let me celebrate their lives and
encourage them. Today, let me share
a smile and a kind word with all
whom I meet. And, let the love of
Your Son Jesus be reflected
in my care and concern
for others this day and every day.

Amen

Help Me, Lord... To Follow Your Will

Teach me to do thy will; for thou art my God: thy Spirit is good; lead me into the land of uprightness.

Psalm 143:10 KJV

God has will, and so do we. He gave us the power to make choices for ourselves, and He created a world in which those choices have consequences. The ultimate choice that we face, of course, is what to do about God. We can cast our lot with Him by choosing Jesus Christ as our personal savior, or not. The choice is ours alone.

We also face thousands of small choices that make up the fabric of daily life. When we align those choices with God's commandments, and when we align our lives with God's will, we receive His abundance, His peace, and His joy. But when we struggle against God's will for our lives, we reap a bitter harvest indeed.

Today, you'll face thousands of small choices; as you do, use God's Word as your guide. And, as you face the ultimate choice, place God's Son and God's will and God's love at the center of your life. You'll discover that God's plan is far grander than any you could have imagined.

Oh Lord, let me not live to be useless.

John Wesley

Most of us go through life praying a little, planning a little, jockeying for position, hoping but never being quite certain of anything, and always secretly afraid that we will miss the way. This is a tragic waste of truth and never gives rest to the heart. There is a better way. It is to repudiate our own wisdom and take instead the infinite wisdom of God.

A. W. Tozer

Get into the habit of dealing with God about everything.

Oswald Chambers

Doing God's will is never hard. The only thing that is hard is not doing His will.

Oswald Chambers

Today's Prayer

Dear Lord, You are the Creator of the universe, and I know that Your plan for my life is grander than I can imagine. Let Your purposes be my purposes. Let Your will be my will. When I am confused, give me clarity. When I am worried, give me strength. Let me be Your faithful servant, Lord, always seeking Your guidance and Your will for my life. Let me live this day and every day according to Your commandments and with the assurance of Your promises, in Jesus' name I pray.

Amen

And
In Conclusion...

Abundance...

...these things I speak in the world, that they might have my joy fulfilled in themselves.

John 17:13 KJV

I am come that they might have life, and that they might have it more abundantly.

John 10:10 KJV

Commit to the Lord whatever you do, and your plans will succeed.

Proverbs 16:3 NIV

But as for you, be strong and do not give up, for your work will be rewarded.

II Chronicles 15:7 NIV

His lord said unto him, Well done, thou good and faithful servant: thou hast been faithful over a few things, I will make thee ruler over many things: enter thou into the joy of thy lord.

Matthew 25:21 KJV

Accepting Christ...

For God so loved the world, that he gave his only begotten Son, that whosoever believeth in him should not perish, but have everlasting life.

John 3:16 KJV

For the wages of sin is death, but the gift of God is eternal life in Christ Jesus our Lord.

Romans 6:23 NIV

He saved us, not on the basis of deeds which we have done in righteousness, but according to His mercy, by the washing of regeneration and renewing by the Holy Spirit, whom He poured out upon us richly through Jesus Christ our Savior....

Titus 3:5-6 NASB

Jesus answered and said unto her, Whosoever drinketh of this water shall thirst again: but whosoever drinketh of the water that I shall give him shall never thirst; but the water that I shall give him shall be in him a well of water springing up into everlasting life.

John 4:13-14 KJV

God Calls Upon Us to Turn Away from Anger...

A patient man has great understanding,
but a quick-tempered man displays folly.
Proverbs 14:29 NIV

But I tell you that anyone who is angry with
his brother is subject to judgment.
Matthew 5:22 NIV

Make no friendship with an angry man....
Proverbs 22-24 KJV

Refrain from anger and turn from wrath;
do not fret—it leads only to evil.
Psalm 37:8 NIV

...do not let the sun go down on your anger, and
do not give the devil an opportunity.
Ephesians 4:26-27 NASB

God's Way...

He will teach us his ways. so that
we may walk in his paths.

Isaiah 2:3 NIV

But I say to you, love your enemies, and
pray for those who persecute you.

Matthew 5:44 NASB

A new commandment I give unto you,
That ye love one another; as I have loved you,
that ye also love one another.

John 13:34 KJV

And just as you want men to treat you,
treat them in the same way.

Luke 6:31 NASB

And we pray this in order that you may live
a life worthy of the Lord and may please him
in every way: bearing fruit in every good work,
growing in the knowledge of God.

Colossians 1:10 NIV

The Cheerful Spirit...

...the cheerful heart has a continual feast.

Proverbs 15:15 NIV

A cheerful heart is good medicine, but
a crushed spirit dries up the bones.

Proverbs 17:22 NIV

Delight thyself also in the LORD; and
he shall give thee the desires of thine heart.

Psalm 37:4 KJV

Verily, verily, I say unto you, Whatsoever
ye shall ask the Father in my name, he will
give it you. Hitherto have ye asked nothing in
my name: ask, and ye shall receive, that
your joy may be full.

John 16:23-24 KJV

I will thank you, Lord with all my heart;
I will tell of all the marvelous things you have
done. I will be filled with joy because of you.
I will sing praises to your name, O Most High.

Psalm 9:1-2 NLT

Courtesy...

Use hospitality one to another
without grudging.

I Peter 4:9 KJV

A soft answer turneth away wrath:
but grievous words stir up anger.

Proverbs 15:1 KJV

A kind man benefits himself, but
a cruel man brings trouble on himself.

Proverbs 11:17 NIV

Be gentle unto all men, apt to teach, patient.

II Timothy 2:24 KJV

And be ye kind one to another, tenderhearted,
forgiving one another, even as God for
Christ's sake hath forgiven you.

Ephesians 4:32 KJV

Encouraging Others...

But encourage one another day after day, as long as it is still called "Today," so that none of you will be hardened by the deceitfulness of sin.

Hebrews 3:13 NASB

Feed the flock of God which is among you....

I Peter 5:2 KJV

Let the word of Christ dwell in you richly in all wisdom; teaching and admonishing one another in psalms and hymns and spiritual songs, singing with grace in your hearts to the Lord.

Colossians 3:16 KJV

Be kindly affectioned one to another with brotherly love; in honor preferring one another; not slothful in business; fervent in spirit; serving the Lord; rejoicing in hope; patient in tribulation; continuing instant in prayer....

Romans 12:10-12 KJV

...I tell you the truth, whatever you did for one of the least of these brothers of mine, you did for me.

Matthew 25:40 NIV

About Faith...

Now faith is the substance of things hoped for, the evidence of things not seen.

Hebrews 11:1 KJV

For verily I say unto you, That whosoever shall say unto this mountain, Be thou removed, and be thou cast into the sea; and shall not doubt in his heart, but shall believe that those things which he saith shall come to pass; he shall have whatsoever he saith.

Mark 6:23 KJV

Trust in the LORD with all thine heart; and lean not unto thine own understanding. In all thy ways acknowledge him, and he shall direct thy paths.

Proverbs 3:5-6 KJV

I can do everything through him that gives me strength.

Phillippians 4:13 NIV

Cast your burden upon the Lord and He will sustain you: He will never allow the righteous to be shaken.

Psalm 55:22 NASB

Friends...

A friend loves at all times....

Proverbs 17:17 NIV

Thine own friend, and thy father's friend,
forsake not....

Proverbs 27:10 KJV

Happy are those who deal justly with others
and always do what is right.

Psalm 106:3 NLT

In everything, therefore, treat people
the same way you want them to treat you,
for this is the Law and the Prophets.

Matthew 7:12 NASB

As we have therefore opportunity,
let us do good unto all men....

Galatians 6:10 KJV

On Forgiveness...

Blessed are the merciful, for they
will be shown mercy.

Matthew 5:7 NIV

Whenever you stand praying, forgive,
if you have anything against anyone, so
that your Father in heaven will also
forgive you your transgressions.

Mark 11:24 NASB

Praise the Lord, I tell myself, and never forget
the good things he does for me.
He forgives all my sins....

Psalm 103:3 NLT

He that saith he is in the light, and hateth
his brother, is in darkness even until now.

I John 2:9 KJV

Hatred stirs up dissention, but
love covers over all wrongs.

Proverbs 10:12 NIV

Generosity...

Do not withhold good from those who deserve it when it is within your power to act.

Proverbs 3:27 NIV

Freely you have received, freely give.

Matthew 10:8 NIV

He that hath two coats, let him impart to him that hath none; and he that hath meat, let him do likewise.

Luke 3:11 KJV

And let us not be weary in well doing: for in due season we shall reap, if we faint not.

Galatians 6:9 KJV

And above all things have fervent charity among yourselves: for charity shall cover the multitude of sins.

I Peter 4:8 KJV

The Golden Rule...

Therefore all things whatsoever ye would that men should do to you, do ye even so to them: for this is the law and the prophets.

Matthew 7:12 KJV

As we have therefore opportunity, let us do good unto all men, especially unto them who are of the household of faith.

Galatians 6:10 KJV

Be kindly affectioned one to another with brotherly love; in honor preferring one another; not slothful in business; fervent in spirit; serving the Lord; rejoicing in hope; patient in tribulation; continuing instant in prayer....

Romans 12:10-12 KJV

God is love; and he that dwelleth in love dwelleth in God, and God in him.

I John 4:16 KJV

...I tell you the truth, whatever you did for one of the least of these brothers of mine, you did for me.

Matthew 25:40 NIV

On Love…

Though I speak with the tongues of men and
of angels, and have not charity, I am become
as sounding brass, or a tinkling cymbal.

I Corinthians 13:1 KJV

He that loveth his brother abideth in the light,
and there is none occasion
of stumbling in him.

I John 2:10 KJV

Hatred stirs up dissention, but
love covers over all wrongs.

Proverbs 10:12 NIV

A new commandment I give unto you,
That ye love one another;
as I have loved you….

John 13:34 KJV

God is love; and he that dwelleth in
love dwelleth in God, and God in him.

I John 4:16 KJV

God's Peace...

And let the peace of God rule in
your hearts...and be ye thankful.

Colossians 3:15 KJV

Be perfect, be of good comfort, be of one mind,
live in peace; and the God of love and
peace shall be with you.

II Corinthians 13:11 KJV

Return unto thy rest, O my soul; for
the LORD hath dealt bountifully with thee.

Psalm 116:7 KJV

Come to me all you who are weary and
burdened, and I will give you rest. Take
my yoke upon you and learn from me, for
I am gentle and humble in heart, and you will
find rest for your soul. For my yoke is easy
and my burden is light.

Matthew 11:28-30 NIV

Peace I leave with you, my peace I give
unto you: not as the world giveth, give
I unto you. Let not your heart be troubled,
neither let it be afraid.

John 14:27 KJV

About the Author

Criswell Freeman is a Doctor of Clinical Psychology who works and lives in Nashville, Tennessee. Dr. Freeman has written over 50 inspirational books including:

Prayers for the Graduate's Journey
A Time to Grieve... A Time to Heal
Your Grief & God's Promises
When Life Throws You a Curveball, Hit It!
God Can Handle It for Graduates

Dr. Freeman is married, and he has two daughters.